Love Affairs at the Villa Nelle

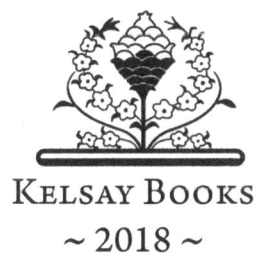

Kelsay Books
~ 2018 ~

Copyright © 2018 individual authors
All rights revert to authors

The Library of Congress has assigned
this edition a Control Number of
2018963647

ISBN 978-1-949229-47-9 (paperback)

Cover image adapted from a photo by Annie Spratt on Unsplash.com

Cover and book design by F. J. Bergmann

Kelsay Books
502 S 1040 E
A119
American Fork, Utah 84003
kelsaybooks.com

First Printing

The Villa Nelle: an Introduction

Welcome, Reader! We thank you heartily for stopping in at the historic *Villa Nelle*—a most agreeable hideaway for admirers of the Villanelle poetic form, where love affairs of every predilection and temperament are celebrated.

Please note that our well-appointed literary suites have been carefully designed to cater to a wide variety of tastes. Scenic vistas abound; and for the more fireside-inclined, thoughtful emotional landscapes are plentiful.

It has all been made possible thanks to the skills and creativity of sixty distinguished Villanelle Personnel—all of whom are listed in the Guest Registry, aka the *Table of Contents*. Each contributor has mastered the villanelle's time-honored conventions (often with compelling variations): nineteen lines in all, only two rhymes from top to bottom, plus a couplet, divided and re-united at pre-arranged moments).

We hope that you will thoroughly enjoy your visit. Please note that well-behaved cats and dogs are always welcome, and refreshments are available to you at the bar. At the end of your stay, a metaphorical chocolate will appear on your pillow.

—*Marilyn L. Taylor & James P. Roberts*

Marilyn L. Taylor, Senior Editor
Former Poet Laureate of Wisconsin, Taylor has published six poetry collections, most recently *Step on a Crack* (Kelsay Books, 2016). Her work has appeared in *Poetry, Measure, Light,* and the Knopf *Everyman's* anthology, *Villanelles*. She has been awarded the international Margaret Reid Poetry Prize, and was a finalist for the X. J. Kennedy Parody Contest, the Howard Nemerov Sonnet Award, and the *Lascaux Review* Prize.

James P. Roberts, Associate Editor
The author of fifteen books in the fields of fantasy and science fiction, poetry, literary biography and baseball history, James is a regional Vice President for the Wisconsin Fellowship of Poets. He lives in Madison, Wisconsin, and is very much involved in the Little Free Library movement. (You may even find a Little Free Library in the Villa Nelle!)

Table of Contents

The Villa Nelle: an Introduction iii

Essential Places, Necessary Things

We Come from the Furnace of the Stars ~ *Lisa Vihos*	3
On a Line from Frost ~ *Catherine Chandler*	4
Remembrances of Yours ~ *Ned Balbo*	5
Trees ~ *Mary Meriam*	6
Lake Michigan Inlet ~ *David Southward*	7
Villanelle on a Line by Plenty Coups ~ *Jennifer Reeser*	8
Joie ~ *Pat Valdata*	9
That Summer ~ *Eileen Mattmann*	10
Record Hound ~ *Paul Creswell*	11
Cyborg Love ~ *Thomas O. Davenport*	12
Second Thoughts ~ *Ed Werstein*	13
Phone Nostalgia ~ *Janet McCann*	14

Children, Cats, and Other Cargo

I Dreamed of Being Mothered by a Cat ~ *Julie Kane*	17
Discovering a Small Headstone by a Path ~ *Karen Kelsay*	18
Circadian Lament, Sung to a Wakeful Baby ~ *Maryann Corbett*	19
Diagnosis: Autism ~ *Barbara Crooker*	20
Lovechildren ~ *Kate Bernadette Benedict*	21
Executive Orders ~ *Judith Terzi*	22
Maurice Utrillo enfant, nu, debout, jouant du pied avec une cuvette ~ *Moira Egan*	23
Loving Otto Plath ~ *Kim Bridgford*	24
The Demon Lovers ~ *Susan McLean*	25
Services ~ *Meredith Bergmann*	26
The Overview ~ *Gail White*	27
Pigeon Lady ~ *Paul Hostovsky*	28

On Mortality

Charlie ~ *Martin Elster*	31
Return Path ~ *Lesley Wheeler*	32
The Last of the Courtyard ~ *Emily Grosholz*	33
Her Things Become Her ~ *Nancy Jesse*	34
Marooned ~ *Melissa Balmain*	35

Demented Carousel ~ *Terese Coe*	36
Dance Lessons ~ *Kathrine Varnes*	37
Impatient ~ *T. A. Cullen*	38
The Owl and the Antelope ~ *Wendy Videlock*	39
For Shadowment: Villanelle for the Solstice ~ *Angela Alaimo O'Donnell*	40
Happy Endings ~ *Richard Merelman*	41
Red & Gold ~ *Chris O'Carroll*	42

On Grief and Loss

Villanelle For Darcy ~ *Jerome Betts*	45
Saudade ~ *Andrew Szilvasy*	46
Slow Finale ~ *Bruce Bennett*	47
To an Old Friend Who Died Young ~ *Michael Cantor*	48
Yesterday ~ *Laurel Devitt*	49
One Kind of Purgatory ~ *Jane Satterfield*	50
What's Left ~ *Brian Jerrold Koester*	51
Two Sisters ~ *Wendy Sloan*	52
Sea Crows ~ *Mary Jo Balistreri*	53
A Housewife ~ *Jeff Holt*	54
Those Things My Mother Said ~ *Burt Myers*	55
Villanelle of the Hunt ~ *Margaret Benbow*	56

On Healing

Requests for Torch Songs for Flowers Sent to the Villanelle Show ~ *Richard Roe*	59
Blues Manqué ~ *Claudia Gary*	60
Tilting Season ~ *Susan Delaney Spear*	61
A Life's Curiosities ~ *Taylor Graham*	62
Ceremony ~ *Debra Bruce*	63
The Villanelle's Villanelle ~ *Anna M. Evans*	64
January Song ~ *Catherine Abbey Hodges*	65
Coming to Terms over Coffee ~ *Leslie Monsour*	66
Supermooning ~ *Amy Lemmon*	67
Backup Plan ~ *A. M. Juster*	68
Clearance ~ *Barbara Loots*	69
Beach of Edges ~ *Annie Finch*	70
The Villanellists	71

Essential Places, Necessary Things

… beads and receipts and dolls and cloths, tobacco crumbs, vases and fringes …

—Gwendolyn Brooks

We Come from the Furnace of the Stars

I and everything I love have come from the furnace of the stars …
　　　　　　　　　　—Barbara Brown Taylor

We come from the furnace of the stars
and in their blazing light we beam.
Together, all this world is ours.

Our lives rain down as showers
and all the waters in all the streams
flow from the furnace of the stars.

And all this love that ever flowers,
tied each to each on threaded seam.
Together, all this world is ours.

In every color, every hour,
every place where dreamers dream—
we come from the furnace of the stars.

Rise up in truth to power
and do not fear its grimy gleam.
Together, all this world is ours.

With voices raised, we tower!
We care, we share, we are, we seem.
Together, all this world is ours.
We come from the furnace of the stars.

　　　　　　　　　　Lisa Vihos

On a Line from Frost

From Pennsylvania she has traveled far,
yet home is in the valley and the hills.
She loves the things she loves for what they are.

The watchful moon once tracked a Pullman car
past dingy culm banks and the linen mills
of Pennsylvania. She has traveled far,

slept under Crux's blue-white triple star,
spent lavish pesos, pink two-dollar bills,
and loved. Some things she loves for where they are

and are not—dyads on a steel guitar—
her landscapes, be they Uruguay's, Brazil's
or Pennsylvania's. Though she's traveled far,

she's always thought in terms of *au revoir*,
a promise that—if dreams count—she fulfills.
Those souls she loved and loves know who they are,

and leaving them behind has left a scar,
a tolerance for pain and sleeping pills.
From Pennsylvania she has traveled far
and wide. She waits. And loves things as they are.

Catherine Chandler

first published in *Line of Flight* (Able Muse Press)

Remembrances of Yours

> *My lord, I have remembrances of yours ...*
> *—Hamlet, 3.1.93*

My love, I have remembrances of yours
to give back now that nothing else remains—
letters or cards delivered to the doors

of homes I lived in long ago, no worse
for so much pained reading between the lines.
Should I return remembrances of yours,

or keep them? Words last; nothing else endures.
Ophelia knew. Each line I read sustains
your presence, ruined memory of doors

that shut behind—between us, back when stars
cluttered the sky with constellations, signs
not meaningless. Remembrances of yours

I can't destroy or throw away, the source
of cadence, rhythm, voice, though paper thins
and letters fade from pages. *All the doors*

of all the lives we'll never lead ... Reverse
the path of stars, see how it all begins—
My love, I hold remembrances of yours—
These words you touched ... The dark behind closed doors.

Ned Balbo

first published in *Per Contra*

Trees

I love this screen of oak and maple trees
hiding me from the boaters on the lake.
I love the fattened leaves in summer's breeze

singing the forest full of symphonies.
When I have any love-life left to make,
I love this screen of oak and maple trees.

When burdened by my sad, old memories,
the screeching hawk, the tick, the lying snake,
I love the fattened leaves in summer's breeze,

their veiny palms and festive shapes, the bees
and hummingbirds that sip them as they shake.
I love this screen of oak and maple trees

the way most people love their families.
For having none, and for my longing's sake,
I love the fattened leaves in summer's breeze.

I listen to the play of green degrees
of pitch and key, the greens the breezes wake
forming this screen of oak and maple trees
bearing the fattened leaves in summer's breeze.

Mary Meriam

Lake Michigan Inlet

Its ripples strum the banks of grassy dunes,
where kids prance in a passing jet ski's wake.
Cooling your feet on summer afternoons,

you try to picture prehistoric Junes—
the glacial force, the eons it must take
for ripples to strum the banks of grassy dunes—

until the echolalia of the loons
reminds you that some truths are too opaque.
Just cool your feet. On summer afternoons

this blue, a kindred blueness in you swoons;
the only thing to do is to partake
in ripples that strum the banks of grassy dunes

and enter—by raft, yacht, kayak, or pontoon—
a basin wide enough to quench your ache
or cool your feet on summer afternoons.

A simple beauty, common as the moon's,
attracts us to the shoals of this Great Lake,
whose ripples strum the banks of grassy dunes
and cool the feet on summer afternoons.

David Southward

Villanelle on a Line by Plenty Coups

"The ground on which we stand is sacred ground,"
The blood of those we love—silt, peat, and sand.
For this, we and our children, too, are bound.

If you must probe it, make your dig profound
In order to find Nature's share of land.
The ground on which we stand is sacred ground.

Our forebears fill its surface. Spin around.
Take up a fistful. Sift it from your hand.
For this, we and our children, too, are bound.

With roots to weave their long braids—parched and browned—
By Burnt Lip and Bad War Deed, they are clanned.
The ground on which we stand is sacred ground.

On this, we dance! The drums of sunlight pound,
As their life forces and their love demand.
For this, we and our children, too, are bound.

Where—other than in wind—may they be found?
Our feet leave an impression like a brand.
The ground on which we stand is sacred ground.
For this, we and our children, too, are bound.

Jennifer Reeser

Joie

Jeanne Labrosse (1775–1847), first woman to fly solo in a hot-air balloon, 1798

I floated over Lyons all alone
It was just as you had promised, *cher,*
My heart was filled with *joie du ballon.*

I could see the whole city of Lyons
With perfect clarity in the morning air
While I floated over Lyons all alone.

I had to shield my eyes against the sun
That shone above the steeples in the square,
My soul transported by *joie du ballon.*

I soared so near to heaven's throne
The awe was almost more than I could bear
As I floated over Lyons all alone.

This vista should be seen by everyone!
I wished more of *mes soeurs* would dare
The thrilling flight of *joie du ballon!*

I knew that soon this flight would be done
And nothing in the future would compare.
My rapture was *tout joie du ballon*
When I floated over Lyons all alone.

Pat Valdata

first published in *Where No Man Can Touch* (West Chester University Poetry Center)

That Summer

There was, with you, a certain *je ne sais quoi,*
a pull, a yearning that poets immortalize—
you dazzled with your cavalier sangfroid.

Those days were fierce, light-filled phenomena.
To friends I hardly saw I'd rhapsodize
That there was only you with your *je ne sais quoi.*

We feasted on bread, wine, and fine foie gras.
Thrumming in the heat, we'd harmonize.
You dazzled with your cavalier sangfroid.

Sun-soaked romantics, we spoke in love's patois,
living in our singular mad paradise.
There was, with you, a certain *je ne sais quoi.*

Did I dance, unknowing, in a *pas de trois?*
Did exuberant love need cutting down to size?
Less dazzling was your cavalier sangfroid.

Heart tattered, I remain *hors de combat,*
the mystery of the gift, I recognize.
There was, with you, a certain *je ne sais quoi.*
I was dazzled by your cavalier sangfroid.

Eileen Mattmann

Record Hound

Take me where I would be found
Drop your jacket to the floor
I'll lay you down and spin you 'round

Your darkened curves are now unbound
That open heart I so adore
Your shiny groove begins to sound

Raise your voice from roof to ground
And I will turn you on once more
You take me where I would be found

Formats shift, and others drown
But you're my anchor and my core
My vinyl ballast, pound for pound

Come, I'll flip you upside-down
Close the windows, lock the door
Out of sight, we'll paint the town

You tease my heart and ease my frown
Eardrums quiver, memories roar
Take me where I would be found
I'll lay you down and spin you 'round

Paul Creswell

Cyborg Love

My cyborg love is Model Q Two Two
Her servomotor hums sweet poetry
It matters not if this seems strange to you

For some, this noise is background buzz on cue
For me, a symphony in minor key
My cyborg love is Model Q Two Two

I see love's beauty in her shiny hue
And I know she sees me in full 3D
It matters not if this seems strange to you

To pledge my troth, a piston ring will do
Her product type lacks fingers, as you see
My cyborg love is Model Q Two Two

Some warn us this won't work—she's "what," I'm "who"
She has no ears, and so can't hear this plea
It matters not if this seems strange to you

Her Romeo, I'm faithful through and through
Though smitten I may be by Q Two Three
For now, my love is Model Q Two Two
It matters not if this seems strange to you

Thomas O. Davenport

Second Thoughts

Above all else on earth I love my guns.
They're symbols of my freedom and my rights.
Each and every citizen should own one.

The deadliest of arms for sale beneath the sun
can put me on the top in any fight.
Above all else on earth I love my guns.

The founding fathers would scratch their heads and wonder why liberal dweebs can't seem to see the light.
Each and every citizen should own one.

On second thought, not each and every one.
Just each and every citizen who's white.
Above all else on earth I love my guns.

Above my wife, my daughters and my sons
whose lives my guns protect throughout the night.
Each and every citizen should own one.

Opposing points of view I always shun.
There's only one amendment I can cite.
Each and every citizen should own one.
Above all else on earth I love my guns.

Ed Werstein

Phone Nostalgia

I liked the way a phone call used to be:
If home, you got it; and if not, then not.
There was no jiggery-pokery—

If the phone rang, it had to be for me.
I could and did ignore it, quite a lot.
But I liked the way a phone call used to be.

I liked the ring, the sheer simplicity.
It was the answerer who called the shot.
There was no jiggery-pokery

Of phone-tag, messages, machinery.
The link was made or missed right on the spot.
I liked the way a phone call used to be.

Someone would call who wished to speak with me
And always human, never some robot.
There was no jiggery-pokery.

No choices, no "Press one, or two, or three."
Never a credit scam or Ponzi plot.
I liked the way a phone call used to be.
There was no jiggery-pokery.

Janet McCann

Children, Cats, and Other Cargo

Eternity in leaps and bounds …

—David Lacey

I Dreamed of Being Mothered by a Cat

I dreamed of being mothered by a cat,
Sunk in her plush as in a featherbed.
I'd never known a happiness like that.

My human mother's claws would not retract.
Even her language could unzipper red.
I dreamed of being mothered by a cat

Who'd give her life to save me from attack.
I sensed that fierceness in her as I fed.
I'd never known a happiness like that.

If there were siblings, I ignored that fact.
I had her to myself (or I forget)
The whole time I was mothered by a cat.

One dream can strike you like a thunderclap.
That mother cat, more goddess than a pet.
I'd never known a happiness like that.

The world was pure sensation, not abstract:
Some realm between the living and the dead.
I dreamed of being mothered by a cat
And something healed inside me after that.

Julie Kane

first published in *2 Bridges Review*

Discovering a Small Headstone by a Path

I saw your tilted headstone by the tree;
A chiseled piece of slate of meager height
Engraved: *To Vic, in loving memory.*

Perhaps a tabby cat or spaniel? We
Have only birth and death dates as insight;
I saw your tilted headstone by the tree.

Out on this large estate, a filigree
Of lime leaves sieve-small specks of autumn light
Across: *To Vic, in loving memory.*

You died at ten, but in reality,
Your spirit is still floating like a kite,
Tied to your tilted headstone by the tree.

Those old aristocrats who sipped their tea,
Bestowed your marker, here, just to the right—
It reads: *To Vic, in loving memory.*

And I, too, mourn a creature, quietly.
The grave, the leaves, all emblems of my plight;
I won't forget your headstone by the tree,
It says: *To Vic, in loving memory.*

Karen Kelsay

Circadian Lament, Sung to a Wakeful Baby

Go back to sleep. You've made a slight mistake
switching your days and nights around this way.
The time will come for nights you spend awake,

for cough and colic, ear- and stomach-ache.
Though now you babble charmingly and play
the infant hours away (a light mistake),

there will be bitter medicines to take
some night. Take love: its wide-eyed thrills one day,
its clammy sweats the next. Take nights awake,

your soul in shreds, your bank account at stake,
your eyelids propped with stale café au lait.
Searching the stars for some obscure mistake

when futures cloud and omens turn opaque
and panic makes you pace the floors and pray—
There will be no escape from nights awake,

I warn you. And my wisdom doesn't make
one whit of difference. *Seize the night,* you say
in coo and babble. Ah, well. My mistake.
Instruct me in the joys of nights awake.

Maryann Corbett

first published in *Tilt-A-Whirl*

Diagnosis: Autism

I'm here to get my baby out of jail:
it's his own mind that's getting in the way.
I will not falter, neither will I fail.

We're on a one-way train that tracks against the rail.
He has no words, or are there none to say?
I'm here to get my baby out of jail.

My time is what I spend to make the bail
and I will give all that it takes to pay.
I will not falter, neither will I fail.

Like trying to drain the ocean with a pail
is how I feel in facing each new day.
I'm here to get my baby out of jail.

He's on the sea in a boat without a sail
or rudder, and must learn to find the way.
I will not falter, neither will I fail.

And though this task is hard and I am frail
and nothing can be done, the doctors say,
I'm here to get my baby out of jail.
I will not falter, neither will I fail.

Barbara Crooker

Lovechildren

My children all have different fathers.
Mom's prolific, blowzy, loose.
My children all have different mothers.

Bikers in their bad-ass leathers,
priests and mystics, Vulcan, Zeus:
my children all have different fathers.

Moods are like unstable weathers;
masks come in and out of use:
my children all have different mothers.

All those mothers! All those others:
bedroom sounds of bliss, abuse.
My children all have different fathers.

Bride of seven bastard brothers,
seer, hooker, clerk, recluse:
My children all have different mothers.

Motley brood, they share each other's
scandal as I reproduce.
My children all have different fathers.
My children all have different mothers.

Kate Bernadette Benedict

Executive Orders

after a photo of Fumiko Hayashida (1911–2014) leaving Bainbridge Island in March of 1942 to be transported to what would become the Manzanar War Relocation Center in California

She wears a stylish hat, a tag on a lapel.
A child in her arms & toy. Bombs fell before.
She wraps up their lives. 9066 compels.

A week to settle the farm, no time to sell.
Layers under coats, one suitcase, not more.
She wears a stylish hat, a tag on a lapel.

Bainbridge Island fades, her berries, her well.
A ferry glides them to the railroad car.
She wraps up their lives. The Order compels.

Her child will not recall how she was held,
the reckless thrall. On the train to Manzanar
she wears a stylish hat, a tag on a lapel.

Walls not done, a son is born in their cell.
Three more years of bombs to end the war.
She wraps up their lives. The Order compels.

Fumiko's now gone, but the lens foretells
what can happen again—disgrace, a scar.
She'll wear a stylish hat, a tag on a lapel.
She'll wrap up their lives. Orders compel.

Judith Terzi

first published in *The Poeming Pigeon*

Maurice Utrillo enfant, nu, debout, jouant du pied avec une cuvette

after the drawing by Suzanne Valadon, 1894

I want to tell him that I know the ache
he feels, the gnawing emptiness,
like hunger, or a thirst that can't be slaked.

It's difficult, those mornings when he wakes
from hot disordered dreams that mar his rest.
I want to tell him that I know the ache,

the looking glass become a muddy lake
of roots obscured, of pure unknowingness,
of hunger, and a thirst that can't be slaked.

It breaks my heart, the jokes the children make,
that small, angelic face cast down in sadness.
I want to say I understand the ache.

He plays his strange distractions, and I take
some comfort that he's soothing loneliness,
the hunger, and the thirst so hard to slake.

But I can't tell him. Is it a mistake
to hold this secret tightly to my breast?
I want to tell him that I feel the ache,
the hunger, and the thirst that can't be slaked.

Moira Egan

first published in *Tilt-A-Whirl*

Loving Otto Plath

She couldn't understand her father gone,
or why he'd leave her. She was only eight.
She thought it cruel—and that, in death, he'd won.

No matter where she was, she meant to win
him back. She chose the archetypal fight.
She couldn't understand her father gone.

The structures are not anything but pattern:
they're not imbued with love, or tears, or sight.
She thought it cruel—and that, in death, he'd won.

She didn't understand the answer written;
her re-interpretation was her fate.
She couldn't understand her father gone,

so pretended he was there. History's rewritten
all the time. Her mortal life was cold with granite.
She thought it cruel—and that, in death, he'd won.

She practiced as if for a competition,
and so it was: she'd not be second-rate.
She couldn't understand her father gone.
She thought it cruel—and that, in death, she'd won.

Kim Bridgford

The Demon Lovers

Even as a teen I should have known
those long-haired boys who sang so well of sin
were mine to see and hear, but not to own.

Every howl of longing, every moan
that made the small hairs prickle on my skin
thrilled me with danger. But I should have known

that nothing crushes like a rolling stone.
The music's over just when you begin
to feel the beat as if it were your own

ecstatic pulse. Together but alone,
taken outside myself and taken in,
I drowned in moonlight. But I should have known

the wild and hungry face that I was shown:
the stranger in the mirror-pool, my twin.
Those boys were lost in mazes of their own—

trapped in a strutting pose they've long outgrown,
imploding from the emptiness within
or dead by twenty-eight. I should have known
that demon loves have demons of their own.

Susan McLean

first published in *The Formalist*

Services

I tried to love your mother, but I can't.
I dream of smashing dishes. To stay sane,
I lock the bathroom door and then I rant

and rave and sob. I cannot tell it slant.
How to forgive the scorn that caused such pain?
I've tried to love your mother. But I can't

forget the years when her regard was scant,
and now we live with her and her disdain.
I lock the bathroom door and then I rant

at Wedgwood and Limoges, how they supplant
the dish that might be loving, if served plain.
I've tried to love your mother's, but I can't.

Her Royal Doulton's lovely, that I grant,
but it would shatter first in my campaign.
I lock the bathroom door, but hear her rant,

and then pretend she didn't, and recant.
I never chipped her Spode! And I maintain,
I tried to love your mother. But I can't.
I'll lock the bathroom door. I'll have my rant.

Meredith Bergmann

The Overview

My greatest love, a Persian cat,
arrived when I was twenty-two.
I wouldn't have expected that

I'd fall in love in seconds flat
with eyes of enigmatic blue.
My greatest love, a Persian cat,

refuted the old caveat:
Cat-love is not, like dog-love, true.
I wouldn't have expected that

she'd choose my lap for habitat,
but year by year her kindness grew.
My greatest love, a Persian cat,

outlasted many a fine male rat
including, my false darling, you.
(I wouldn't have expected that).

And so I find, while working at
My Life and Loves: An Overview,
my greatest love: a Persian cat.
I wouldn't have expected that.

Gail White

Pigeon Lady

"For me they are like the tide,"
says the pigeon lady, and I've a thought
she's keeping one inside,

a rainbow-necked, red-eyed,
pinioned pigeon weeping in her throat:
"For me they are like the tide—

a thousand times I've tried
to wet my fingers, to touch.
Retreating, they keep inside

each other's little struts, they nod
and float away, nod and float
away. For me they are like the tide."

Behind her drizzling side-
long frowns and crumbs the sun is out.
She's keeping one inside

like that feather lodged or tied
in her blue-gray hair. It's there. It can't hide.
"For me they are like the tide."
Cheeping, one's inside.

Paul Hostovsky

On Mortality

this little hat of life, how will I bear to take it off ...

—Ellen Bass

Charlie

You had the borough's loudest bark,
liked a good romp, a sometime brawl.
Now you're lost in a place so dark

you cannot find a tree to mark,
nor a patch of lawn on which to sprawl.
You had the city's lustiest bark,

loved chasing chipmunks in the park,
came running when you heard me call.
Now you're lost in a land so dark

the frisbees wander off their arc.
No odors there, nor even a ball
to fetch. Inside my dreams, you bark

then leap in the rapids on a lark.
The leash I'm grasping snaps as you fall
to the cataract of timeless dark.

I catch a glimpse, a familiar spark
of brown and white. I see you crawl,
roll over, sit—hear one faint bark
from the farthest, darkest land of dark.

Martin Elster

Return Path

The only way to pray is through my feet,
earthward, jolted in return by the fizz
of a spiking current. I never thought a circuit

would loop through me, believed I was separate,
alone, done with gods, but here it is:
I've found a way to pray. Through my feet,

I reach down. There's something animate,
chthonic, that touches me back. It's a species
of love, a thinking-spike, a zinging circuit

of energy and dirt, blood and spirit—
plutonic conversation, mostly wordless.
The way I've found to pray is through my feet,

sole bared to wooden boards, or rug, or slate,
or buggy grass, just as you want to press
skin to a beloved's, sparking a current, a circuit.

Not that earth loves me, exactly. Matter's what
matters. She wants me to return the mess
of my only body, pray from head through feet
as I sink, unthinking ash, into love's circuit.

Lesley Wheeler

The Last of the Courtyard

Who will believe me later, when I say
We lived in a state of music? Passing birds
And mice met on the roof, and danced away.

Francis played his silver flute, and Guy
His violin; the children sang in words.
Who will believe me later, when I say

We lived on little else from day to day?
Life in the courtyard was its own reward.
Mice danced across the roof, and ran away.

Carpenter, painter, potter: poverty
Is the sole good a singing man affords,
Though not at last sufficient. As they say,

We lose the things for which we cannot pay:
Our houses were sold out, over our heads.
Even the dancing mice must go away,

Nothing remains of us but memory,
A fleeting minor air, absently heard.
Who will believe me later, when I say
The mice danced on the roof, and ran away?

Emily Grosholz

first published in *The Hudson Review*

Her Things Become Her

She's been here, and now she's gone,
leaving her mark like an imprint in snow.
Her things are still here, but she has moved on.

I've kept all her books, from Proust to Audubon,
see her freckled hand scribbling notes that show
she had once been here, and now she is gone.

Bundt pans, quiche dishes, molds for bonbon—
she could bake anything, called cake *gâteau*.
Her things are still here, but she has moved on.

In my closet, her clothing—white chiffon,
purple suede, pure silk petticoats—as though
she has just been here, and now she has gone.

I'd call it a bun, but she said *chignon*.
I still have her hair clips, pins and *bandeau*.
Her things are still here, but she has moved on.

When I touch what was hers she returns, for one
moment or two, reminding me. I know
that she has been here. That she is gone.
That what was hers is mine. That she has moved on.

Nancy Jesse

first published in *Wisconsin People & Ideas*

Marooned

Nothing moves us like a person stuck—
a toddler in a well, a stranded scout:
we gather at our screens and pray for luck.

Will storms bypass the climbers? Run amok?
Will all those boaters perish like beached trout?
Nothing moves us like a person stuck,

a coach trapped with his soccer team, their pluck
despite the odds, the rising tide of doubt;
we mourn a diver who ran out of luck

and hold our breath while others roll and tuck
through limestone passages to get them out.
Nothing moves us like a person stuck—

except for seeing (teary, thunderstruck)
the things we've longed for finally come about:
rescues soaked in undiluted luck.

And then we're back to making our next buck,
to swimming after consequence and clout.
Nothing moves us. Like a person stuck,
we peer from caves of bone and pray for luck.

Melissa Balmain

first published in *Rattle*

Demented Carousel

Our days have turned into a carousel,
the tricks and troughs repeating round the bend,
delirious with dizzy oversell.

The temp-to-perms think they're the personnel,
caparisoned with feathers by a friend,
and not mere captives on the carousel.

We'll ride the painted ponies straight to hell!
Whenever someone dies, we all attend,
demented with the drone of oversell,

the funeral forever—we're unwell.
There's no way to alight or comprehend
how we have come to ride the carousel,

and mounted on an ostrich or gazelle,
the riders first decry and then defend
every demented droning oversell,

the senselessness of every bagatelle,
the revolutions round the same dead end,
the calliope and rings on the carousel,
this terminally demented oversell.

Terese Coe

Dance Lessons

They're playing our song, you say. But I can't hear.
I step too quickly, trip, and lose a shoe.
This unlined dress distracts me. Is it sheer?

The tv lurches; you pour down a beer.
The muscle in my chest starts pumping glue.
They're playing our song, you say. But I can't hear.

You smile and joke. I startle from a jeer.
I cannot find a slip that won't show through.
This unlined dress distracts me. Is it sheer

Myth that I descend from Paul Revere
Or maybe someone who shared his North Church pew?
They're playing our song. You say, but I can't hear.

In any case, we all descend; that's clear,
Though twirling tends to skew my point of view.
This unlined dress distracts me. Is it sheer,

This cliff? The doctor blames my inner ear.
Where are the children I meant to have with you?
They're playing our song. You say. But I can't hear;
This unlined dress distracts me. Is it sheer?

Kathrine Varnes

Impatient

Desire ebbs and flows, mostly ebbs these days.
Retired, not in a home yet, like the warehouse
where my sister waits, and prays

in the garden to plant seeds, catch some rays,
relax in the sun, smile at a ghostly spouse.
Desire ebbs and flows, mostly ebbs these days

as does the memory of how he goes and stays
away, has an affair. He was a louse
but my sister waits, and prays

to God, lounges in the sun in her chaise.
He had auburn hair, charm, a bit of a souse
desire ebbs and flows, mostly ebbs these days

my sister lives and pushes through highways
of the home; still it's not the home or house
where my sister waits, and prays

God the Father, Son and Holy Ghost—she says
Set me free, fly like a bird, let me out of this house.
Desire ebbs and flows, mostly ebbs these days
where my sister waits, and prays.

T. A. Cullen

The Owl and the Antelope

The owl and the antelope are seen
to be the prophets, and the subtle notes
where all the earthly dreams have come to dream.

In climates where the written word is deemed
another river mystery, there floats
the owl and the antelope; there is seen

the wizardry of holy gold and green,
for I have been aboard the willow boats
where all the earthly dreams have come to dream.

The panther and the crow reside between
the certainty of seas and distant slopes—
the owl and the antelope are seen

to be where silent sorcery is gleaned
of latent miracles and horoscopes
where all the earthly dreams have come to dream.

The greying wolf and elephant convene
where grief and memory are mighty oaks.
The owl and the antelope are seen
where all the earthly dreams have come to dream.

Wendy Videlock

first published in *Think*

For Shadowment: Villanelle for the Solstice

Here, here in the crook of the year,
the crux and fix and flux of the year
light falls long across and dear.

Here in the ruck and dreck of the year
we glean and gather grace and gear,
here, here in the crook of the year.

Here is the neckbone of the year,
its knuckle sharp, its blade sheer,
where light falls long across and dear.

Hear the matins of the year,
the chant of praise and marrow fear,
here, here in the crook of the year.

Cheer the vespers of the year,
the prayers that rise from tongue to ear
as light falls long across and dear.

Clear your mind as night draws near.
Stead your heart and shed no tear.
Here, here in the crook of the year
where light falls long across and dear.

Angela Alaimo O'Donnell

first published in *The Christian Century*

Happy Endings

Pastrami stacked on pumpernickel rye
is juicy, tangy, chewy. It wouldn't be
the go-to-food for guys about to die

from writing monographs on Philippi
or scanning cantatas. Literati flee
pastrami stacked on pumpernickel rye;

to eat such fatty meat might signify
a hundred vulgar tastes. I crave a deli
and its go-to-food for guys about to die

from forty years of barely getting by
composing jingles (i. e., guys like me).
Pastrami stacked on pumpernickel rye

satisfies the hunger that doesn't lie
about its lust for stuff that's fleshy, heavy,
go-to-food. For guys about to die,

I'd hang the healthy diets out to dry.
More men would say goodbye ecstatically:
pastrami stacked on pumpernickel rye,
the go-to-food for guys about to die.

Richard Merelman

Red & Gold

Flamboyantly decked out in red and gold—
Mellow and misty, yes, but something more—
The year grows gaudier as it grows old.

Before warm breath succumbs to winter cold,
Motley appears from a defiant store
Of finery, flamboyant red and gold.

This late extravagance was not foretold
By all the brilliant boutonnieres spring wore.
The year grows gaudier as it grows old.

Summer's mature green kept a steady hold,
Serenely continent awhile before
Fall's carnival excess of red and gold.

Threescore and more around the sun I've rolled.
Now autumn's frenzy calls me to explore
A madcap gaudiness as I grow old.

That bell time tolls will soon enough be tolled.
I'm primed for this unsubtle metaphor,
For some flamboyant notes of red and gold
To lend a gaudy grace to growing old.

Chris O'Carroll

On Grief and Loss

It will be the past / and we'll live there together …

—Patrick Phillips

Villanelle For Darcy

for C. G. A.

Darcy the diabetic cat has died
His fans were told by email recently,
A life remembered with no little pride.

The Fiat-driver now feels mortified
To think because he simply failed to see
Darcy, the diabetic cat has died.

Was this the fatal ninth and last he'd tried?
Whichever, it will surely prove to be
A life remembered with no little pride.

His poor squashed frame has been discreetly fried
With all involved expressing sympathy:
Darcy the diabetic cat has died.

The people in his road could not abide
The flattening of such fine felinity,
A life remembered with no little pride.

So, some of them sent cards, and others cried
And stuck a sign upon his favourite tree:
Darcy the diabetic cat has died,
A life remembered with no little pride.

Jerome Betts

first published in *Snakeskin* (UK)

Saudade

You grow nostalgic every now and then
for madeleines and tea. You know that Proust's
prose talents far exceed your own

but you're working on your book again,
the memoir of your journey to the west,
for which you grow nostalgic now and then

though the best parts of it were done by friends
you've interviewed in hopes that you'll produce
an engaging work of stories not your own.

Your job's prevented travel and you've grown
so tired of petty chores. But when you're pressed
by peers, you grow nostalgic now and then

for the libraries and dust that kept you in
when friends sat at Fenway and you wrote of Faust.
The dissertation's key points aren't your own

but cobbled thoughts of other scholars. You're alone
and friends have memories and smiles. You've deduced
that what you feel is not nostalgia. Now
you know: the life you've lived is not your own

Andrew Szilvasy

Love Affairs AT THE VILLA NELLE

Slow Finale

I could not hold you; could not let you go.
You waited silently for me to act.
You waited patiently. I did not know

Which way to turn. I eddied in the flow,
snagged in the current, foundered on the fact.
I could not hold you; could not let you go.

My circling was mindless, endless, slow,
although my sense and senses were intact.
I maundered helplessly. I did not know

How to approach you. Beg forgiveness? Throw
myself about, disclosing what I lacked?
I could not hold you; could not let you go;

Could not explain. I watched you puzzle, grow
restless and distant, consciously retract,
no longer patient. Still, I did not know

The curtain was descending on our show;
your train was on its way; your bags were packed.
I could not hold you; could not let you go.
Our play was over, and I did not know.

Bruce Bennett

first published in *Harpur Palate*

To an Old Friend Who Died Young

The first time was a game, we all agreed,
a cry for help, of course, but nothing more
and then you dove out over 87th Street.

The maid was due at noon—you gambled she'd
smell gas as soon as she came near the door—
that first time was a game. We all agreed

you missed your ex; you shrugged, you blamed the weed
and promised us there would be no encore—
but then you broke apart on 87th Street

that Sunday morning. What voices did you heed,
what madness crept up to the 14th floor?
The first time was a game, we all agreed;

we spoke of how you always seemed to need
attention; called up stunts you'd staged before—
and then you sailed out over 87th Street,

and gave the game an ending guaranteed
to make it clear who kept the final score.
The first time was a game, we all agreed;
and then you plummeted to 87th Street.

Michael Cantor

first published in *Lucid Rhythms*

Yesterday

Today marks the first since my last day with you.
My feet hit the floor at the side of the bed.
The sun blinks astounded, the sky winks mad blue.

I smell coffee brewing. I brewed it for two.
I wake up the cats trying to sleep on the spread.
Today marks the first since my last day with you.

The cats sniff around, they are missing you too.
I lift them down lightly, I tell them you've fled.
The sun blinks astounded, the sky winks mad blue.

I sit at the table with the coffee for two.
The cats rub my shins, purring what stays unsaid.
Today marks the first since my last day with you.

My body's ashiver, I need to find shoes.
The skin of the cats shudder rolls from the head.
The sun blinks astounded, the sky winks mad blue.

I gaze at the papers that don't carry the news.
The news that you've gone and the cats must be fed.
The sun blinks astounded, the sky winks mad blue.
Today marks the first since my last day with you.

Laurel Devitt

One Kind of Purgatory

> The inquest into the deaths of Princess Diana and Dodi Al Fayed has seen CCTV footage of their last day together. Here, the couple walk across the lobby of the Ritz in Paris.
> —In Pictures: The Diana Inquest, BBC News, 11 October 2007

It spins again, the revolving door—
The princess & her escort, their hired car ...
What is the camera looking for—

The driver? He tips off the camera corps,
drink in hand, then lingers at the bar.
It spins again, the revolving door—

while those who knew her write memoir.
All's fair, they say, *in love and war.*
What is the camera looking for?

The evidence to settle someone's score?
Ten years on, her death still seems bizarre.
It spins again, the revolving door—

I won't watch the footage anymore.
The chase, two young lives reduced to carnage—
What is the camera looking for,

panning across the stagey Ritz décor
where lovers pause, eager to flee, ill-starred?
It spins forever, the revolving door—
What is the camera—what are we—looking for?

Jane Satterfield

What's Left

What's left of him is boxed up in the ground.
He asked a favor of a secret gun.
The world is not right without him around.

His hair was clean and still combed when they found
him, like he had to go and meet someone.
What's left of him is boxed up in the ground.

His eye flatlined on green. The blue that wound
around it, that our mother loved, has run.
The world is not right without him around.

The clucking about wrong was softly drowned.
A better way? No one was sure of one.
What's left of him is boxed up in the ground.

Beside his grave his children made a sound
like doves, their time with Daddy flown. All done.
The world is not right without him around.

He thought he'd cause less harm there underground
than here above it, but he's snuffed the sun.
What's left of him is boxed up in the ground.
The world is not right without him around.

Brian Jerrold Koester

Two Sisters

She still forgets to lock her kitchen door.
A life-long habit doesn't go away
though no one comes to visit anymore.

In time for morning coffee, or before,
her sister would come over every day,
so she forgets to lock her kitchen door.

On summer days, they'd munch the sour store
of gooseberries, and dish the hours away.
But no one comes to visit anymore.

It's over seven years now since they bore
her sister to the cemetery bay.
Still, she neglects to lock her kitchen door.

The oven's cold now, and the soiled floor
can go without a washing one more day
as no one comes to visit anymore.

And whether they will reach that shaded shore
or meet only in visions, who can say?
She still forgets to lock her kitchen door
though no one comes to visit anymore.

Wendy Sloan

Love Affairs AT THE VILLA NELLE

Sea Crows

Something tethered finally breaks free
in dusk's green gathering. Boats arc west.
Crows stir sunlight that falls to the sea.

Quiet descends on my balcony—
slows my breath, unties knots in my chest,
lets tears surface, at last break free.

The mind can shield, preserve with ennui,
masking emotions one can't digest.
Crows shake the sun's late light in the sea.

In silence, rage below pain is seen,
no longer buried—admitted, addressed.
The thought that life is unfair breaks free.

My daughter's disease consumes by degree,
wrests life from her like a fiend obsessed.
Crows shift the light; bring insight to me.

It changes nothing, but I want to scream
at God, the world—her life's unexpressed.
Tethered by death, she cannot break free.
Crows drop the sun's last light in the sea.

Mary Jo Balistreri

A Housewife

She cleans the tidy house when he's not there,
Restless as memories best left alone,
And tells herself he's learning how to care.

Dusting, she dreams he will caress her hair,
Stroking her curls, praising how long they've grown.
He is so sensitive when he's not there.

Once home, he sprawls out in his leather chair
And yells at her to get the telephone.
She does, thinking he's learning how to care,

He's just a man, and life is never fair.
Such phrases, muttered in Mom's monotone,
Pace through her mind like monks when he is there.

That night, beneath him, trembling like a hare,
She feels him penetrate her, hears him groan,
And tells herself he's learning how to care.

Her life with him is an unquestioned prayer
Chanted against an ominous unknown.
She cleans the tidy house when he's not there
And tells herself he's learning how to care.

Jeff Holt

first published in *Cumberland Poetry Review*

Those Things My Mother Said

I won't forget those things my mother said,
or how she startled to the sky each time
a flock of geese was passing overhead,

forever looking up and out ahead
and making some new mountain hers to climb.
I won't forget. Those things my mother said,

they led to this eccentric life. They led,
but all too rarely, to the wild sublime—
a flock of geese, soon passing. Overhead,

the fowl are gone. The firmament has spread
its mantle. Day turns on a goddamn dime.
I won't. Forget these things. My mother said

that time had sprung, and from her fevered bed,
she could but watch the world receding. I'm
a flock of geese just passing overhead,

now pressing on too fast, my mother dead
and in the ground, as funeral bells chime.
I won't forget the things my mother said—
a flock of geese just passing overhead.

Burt Myers

Villanelle of the Hunt

A river of fur runs through the land.
Red fox leaps high but he dies down low.
If you've never been hunted, you can't understand

how knifes the bullet and clubs the hand:
grin teeth, break bone, strike head the doe:
a river of fur runs through the land.

Great oaks root through our hearts of sand,
red sumac shines through red blood sowed.
If you've never been hunted, you can't understand

how *place to hide* preserves the clan.
Lack that, lack all. This sight behold:
a river of fur runs through the land.

So quick they turn, the animal band,
but bullet knows they can be slowed.
If you've never been hunted, you can't understand

how a stone cold drop of lead commands
this hot flight desperate, death-bestrode.
A river of fur runs through the land.
If you've never been hunted, you can't understand.

Margaret Benbow

On Healing

I'll not, carrion comfort, Despair, nor feast on thee ...

—Gerard Manley Hopkins

Requests for Torch Songs for Flowers Sent to the Villanelle Show

Forget fruitfulness, play me ballads of Lobelia,
let red petals and blue retune my mind,
ease my pain with part-songs for Delphinia.

Croon my Hawkweed in orange, jazz diva Diana,
send me vocal bouquets, I am lame and half-blind.
Forget fruitfulness, spin me ballads for Lobelia.

Like Princess Anastasia, you are lost, Potentilla,
my voice wobbles in search of bloody rhymes,
ease my pain with part-songs for Delphinia.

Play the blues for Bird's Foot Violets, Virginia
Bluebells, Swamp Marigold, nuts to gourds and vines,
forget fruitfulness, play me ballads of Lobelia.

Air it out, get a buzz on, *Apis mellifora*,
scat on Pasqueflowers, melodious Lizz Wright,
ease my pain with part-songs of Delphinia.

Oh, Tierney Sutton, warble for *Narcissus jonquilla*,
please, Miss Villanelle, I'm feeling so low tonight,
Forget fruitfulness, play me ballads for Lobelia,
Ease my pain, play me part-songs for Delphinia.

Richard Roe

Blues Manqué

I've suffered, but I can't quite sing the blues.
My troubles are occasional, not chronic.
My angst is true, but not the kind you'd use

against the everyday, to find or lose
your heart. My chords are major and harmonic.
I've suffered, but I don't dare sing the blues.

Any attempt would probably amuse,
but not in ways your songs have made iconic.
Your angst is true, while mine's nothing to use

in threatening to blow a major fuse
or skip to Paris on the supersonic.
I've not suffered enough to sing the blues.

Saying I have is asking for a bruise.
You'll throw tomatoes. They'll be hydroponic.
This angst is true, but nothing I can use

to make you say mine is the pain you'd choose.
The plates I spin are porcelain, not tectonic.
I suffer from a need to sing the blues
with insufficient angst, too kind to use.

Claudia Gary

first published in *Angle Poetry Journal* (UK)

Tilting Season

February ached with words and wine.
Our poems filled the arid winter season
with Cabernet, Merlot, and rich, red rhyme.

A halting phrase became a lovely line.
Our stanzas brimmed with meaning, but lacked reason,
and I grew tipsy on the words and wine.

Erratic meter was a danger sign,
but I still flirted with the heart of treason;
I sipped her syllables and drank her rhyme.

I lost my step, pretending I was fine,
And stumbled through that tilting winter season,
Intoxicated on the words and wine.

Each week the verse grew stronger, line by line,
A siren's song usurped me of my reason.
I drank poetic nectar, slant on rhyme.

Clarity will visit me in time,
But now, another syllable, oh please, one
More aching word, another glass of wine.
More Cabernet, Merlot, imperfect rhyme.

Susan Delaney Spear

A Life's Curiosities

My day-book's filled with sketches, poems, notes—
the biggest live-oak that I've ever seen,
and how a feather on still air just floats,

and where the bird went; sun-gold's dusty motes,
and storm-clouds just beyond horizon's screen.
My day-book's filled with sketches, poems, notes

I'd jot, watching my dog in bows of boats
or head-high scanning; eyes and nose so keen,
and how a feather on still air just floats

and dreams its way from flight to earth; wild oats
turned platinum on a hill so lately green.
My day-book's filled with sketches, poems, notes—

you'd say, just curious, old anecdotes:
the monkeyflower favors serpentine,
a downy feather on still air just floats.

This is my album, brief spring's chorus-notes,
life passing quicker than the peregrine.
My day-book filled with sketches, poems, notes
and how a feather on still air just floats.

Taylor Graham

Love Affairs AT THE VILLA NELLE

Ceremony

I found a way to bring the rug upstairs.
I roll it up, then tug its heavy body.
I'm rearranging the rooms we used to share.

To slide it across the floor would take me years,
so I stand it up and let it lean on me,
shuffling with it toward the basement stairs.

Oh heavy mate—and who will greet me there?
—to usher in the new reality
of rearranging the rooms we used to share.

You wore a jacket I'd never seen you wear,
moving your things out, keeping your back to me.
I lose my grip, starting up the stairs,

but I don't fall. The rug slides down and flares
apart, away from me, deep burgundy.
I'm rearranging the rooms we used to share.

I don't know why I can't just leave it where
we stashed it away—for good, apparently.
I found a way to drag it back upstairs.
I'm rearranging the rooms we used to share.

Debra Bruce

first published in *Survivors' Picnic* (WordTech Editions)

The Villanelle's Villanelle

I slept for several hours, but didn't dream
of you at all. Perhaps we're finally through
and things are much more fluid than they seem.

Just take the villanelle itself, the cream
of French repeating forms. I thought I knew
its history, but that was just a dream

invented by Victorians, a team
of men who made up rules and called them true,
when things are much more fluid than they seem.

Maybe I made you up? I see a gleam
of Sylvia in everything I do.
I couldn't sleep for hours, and next a dream

seduced me swiftly with its gentle theme
of dying. Then on waking I was blue.
Yet things are much more fluid than they seem.

And though it wasn't really in my scheme
I must confess the truth of losing you:
you weren't my turtledove. You were a dream.
All things are much more fluid than they seem.

Anna M. Evans

January Song

The holidays are over. Now we're here
amidst the candle stubs and bits of ribbon.
Perhaps this stillness is a new career.

The kids had risen early, packed their gear,
made their farewells and then away they'd driven.
The holidays are over. We're still here

after waving from the porch as from a pier
at little crafts on course for the horizon.
Perhaps this stillness is a new career.

Time's origami has its way with fear,
with loss, bright things gone dark and plans gone riven.
The holidays are over. We're left here,

our failures folded into something dear
and strange and new, for which we haven't striven.
This stillness may become a new career.

Old age is coming, but it's not yet near.
These early afterhours are their own heaven.
A certain party's over; now we're here.
Today this stillness is a new career.

Catherine Abbey Hodges

first published as "January Villanelle" in *Connotation Press: An Online Artifact*

Coming to Terms over Coffee

I'd never fall in love with you.
Love fizzles out and mortifies.
Affection's fine, and it will do.

Besides, love's common as bamboo
And flits about like butterflies.
How could I fall in love with you

And send you flowery billets-doux
Or hit upon you otherwise?
Affection's fine, and it will do.

Lovers are fickle and untrue;
They tell each other little lies.
I'd never fall in love with you,

Stoop to some secret rendezvous,
And be reduced to quivering sighs:
Affection's fine, and it will do.

So pour your famous, foreign brew,
As dark and jolting as your eyes.
I'll never fall in love with you;
Affection's fine, and it will do.

Leslie Monsour

Supermooning

We craned to see the sumptuous supermoon
That drizzled on the foggy foreign sky.
It burned and sizzled on and on till noon.

You called from Massachusetts, much too soon—
You haven't just moved on. The spellbound try
And crane to see the scrumptious supermoon.

Emoji hearts don't hold the same balloon,
Confetti brings me down. Could that be why
It burned and sizzled on and on till noon

And stirred the frozen sea? I fought to tune
My inner carburetor's wiring guy.
We craned to see the unctuous supermoon

In separate states, in separate cloudstruck scenes.
I didn't press "send" at first, but by and by
The message burned and sizzled on till noon.

When suddenly my heart, that freeze-dried prune,
Began to thaw and soften. Mollified,
We craned to see. Rambunctious supermoon,
pray burn and sizzle on till long past noon.

Amy Lemmon

Backup Plan

If I were single once again
(not that I'm really planning, dear),
I would indulge! Like other men,

I'd bag the low-fat regimen
and live on burgers, ribs and beer.
If I were single, once again

there would be Fritos in the den,
and napkin rings would disappear.
I would indulge like other men,

not shave or floss, and sleep past ten.
My feelings could be insincere.
If I were single once again,

and free to leave the seat up when
my heart desired, it is clear
I would indulge like other men—

although I *would* be helpless then,
and yearn for your return. I fear
if I were single once again,
I would indulge like other men.

A. M. Juster

first published in *Light*

Clearance

You love these red ones with the four-inch heel.
Just take them down and try them on for size.
Whoa! Wouldn't *those* enhance your sex appeal!

And at a closeout price. Boy—what a steal!
But wait a minute. Wonder if it's wise
to take the risk. Red shoes? A four-inch heel?

When you consider they could make you feel
unsteady as a drunk, you'd compromise
your safety. And for what? Your sex appeal?

A broken ankle is a bad ordeal
at your age, girl. And still you fantasize
risqué potential in a four-inch heel?

You think a shoe will do the trick? Get real.
Your dancing days are done with darling guys
attracted by your brains and sex appeal.

Except they weren't. Youth wasn't that ideal.
You can amuse yourself with harmless lies.
But don't forget the creep. The clod. The heel.
You know there's more to life than sex appeal.

Barbara Loots

Beach of Edges

A drift of snow edges a new drift of sand
As edges grow deeper. It's March, month of edges.
Wet rocks yield to pebbles like opening hands.

The glisten of rockweed trails, splutters, and bends,
And sparkles of rivulets bounce down in ledges.
A drift of snow edges a new drift of sand;

It's March, month of edges, and I'm left to stand
Alone outside time as new light pulls and nudges
Wet rocks. Yield to pebbles like opening hands,

Light; pull me from winter. How have I planned
For light that's not winter, for live light that fledges
A drift of snow, edges a new drift of sand

Beyond my last sight, and waves me like a wand
Out back over the surges of these rocking sedges?
Wet rocks yield to pebbles like opening hands;

I want to go back to him, as to the land;
light, carry me over from the wild old grudges.
A drift of snow edges a new drift of sand;
Wet rocks yield to pebbles like opening hands.

Annie Finch

first published in *Spells: New and Selected Poems* (Wesleyan University Press)

The Villanellists

Ned Balbo's latest book is *3 Nights of the Perseids* (University of Evansville Press), selected by Erica Dawson for the 2018 Richard Wilbur Award.

Mary Jo Balistreri is the author of four poetry books. *Still* was recently published by Future Cycle Press. In addition to writing, she enjoys participating in reading events, and the dialogue that follows.

Melissa Balmain edits the light-verse journal *Light*. Her poetry collection *Walking in on People* (winner of the Able Muse Book Award) is often mistaken by online shoppers for porn.

Kate Bernadette Benedict is the author of *Earthly Use: New and Selected Poems* (2015) and other works. She edited the journals *Umbrella* and *Tilt-a-Whirl*; the archives are linked at katebenedict.com.

Margaret Benbow's poems have appeared in *The Georgia Review*, *Triquarterly*, and *The Ekphrastic Review*. She also writes fiction. Her collection *Boy Into Panther and Other Stories* won the Many Voices Project award from New Rivers Press.

Bruce Bennett's most recent book, *Just Another Day in Just Our Town Poems: New and Selected, 2000–2016*, contains numerous villanelles. He is Professor Emeritus of English at Wells College.

Jerome Betts edits *Lighten Up Online* in Devon, England. His work has appeared in *Amsterdam Quarterly*, *Angle*, *Autumn Sky Poetry Daily*, *Better than Starbucks*, *Light*, *The Rotary Dial*, and *Snakeskin*.

Meredith Bergmann is a sculptor, a widely published poet, and was poetry editor of *American Arts Quarterly* 2006–2017. Her chapbook *A Special Education* was published in 2014 by EXOT Books.

Kim Bridgford is the editor of *Mezzo Cammin* and director of Poetry by the Sea. The author of twelve books, she has received NEA and Ucross Foundation grants.

Debra Bruce's most recent book is *Survivors' Picnic*. Her poems are in current or forthcoming issues of *Innisfree Poetry Journal*, *Shenandoah*, *Tar River Poetry*, and *Valparaiso Poetry Review*. debrabrucepoet.com

Michael Cantor, a native New Yorker, has now gone to ground in Santa Fe (winters) and Massachusetts (summers). His collection *Life in the Second Circle* was a Massachusetts Poetry Award finalist.

Catherine Chandler is the author of *Lines of Flight*, *This Sweet Order*, *Glad and Sorry Seasons*, and *The Frangible Hour*. She lives and writes in Saint-Lazare, Québec, and Punta del Este, Uruguay.

Terese Coe's poems have appeared in *Agenda*, *Cincinnati Review*, *Ploughshares*, *Poetry*, *Poetry Review*, *Threepenny Review*, and the *TLS*. Her collection *Shot Silk* was listed for the 2017 Poets Prize.

Maryann Corbett is the author of four books, most recently, *Street View*, and a winner of the Richard Wilbur Book Award and the Willis Barnstone Translation Prize.

Paul Creswell is a poet, musician, scientist, and record lover based in Madison, Wisconsin. When he's not otherwise occupied, he enjoys a copacetic round of croquet. paulcreswell.com

Barbara Crooker is the author of nine books of poetry; including *Some Glad Morning* (UPitt, 2019). Her work has appeared widely, from *The Bedford Introduction to Literature* to *Commonwealth: Contemporary Poets on Pennsylvania*.

T. A. Cullen is a poet who lives in Madison, Wisconsin. He has had numerous poems published in the *Wisconsin Poets' Calendars* and other publications.

Thomas O. Davenport is an independent writer and business advisor living in San Francisco. He writes verse, much of it sardonic, about social phenomena that amuse and bemuse him.

Laurel Devitt lives and writes in La Crosse, Wisconsin. The bluffs and rivers are inspiration to artists in any medium. She enjoys writing in form. The villanelle is her favorite.

Moira Egan's most recent books are *Olfactorium* (Italic Pequod, 2018) and *Synæsthesium*, which won *The New Criterion* Poetry Prize (2017). She teaches creative writing and lives in Rome.

Martin Elster has known both the joys and the sorrows of canine companionship, inspiring numerous poems. His elderly rat terrier is, indeed, endowed with a truly commanding voice.

Anna M. Evans gained her MFA from Bennington, and teaches at West Windsor Art Center and Rowan College at Burlington County, New Jersey. Her latest book is *Under Dark Waters: Surviving the Titanic*.

Annie Finch's most recent books are *Spells: New and Selected Poems* and *A Poet's Craft*. She co-edited the anthology *Villanelles* from Everyman's Library.

Claudia Gary, author of *Humor Me*, chapbooks, tonal songs, and chamber music, teaches villanelles at The Writer's Center (writer.org) and elsewhere. See pw.org/content/claudia_gary. Follow @claudiagary.

Taylor Graham is a SAR dog handler and El Dorado County's first poet laureate (2016–18); Her work is included in the anthologies *Villanelles* and *California Poetry: From the Gold Rush to the Present*.

Emily Grosholz is a poet and philosopher. Her seventh book of poetry is *The Stars of Earth: New and Selected Poems*. Her book *Childhood* has raised over $3,500 for UNICEF. Her new book on poetry and mathematics, *Great Circles*, is just out from Springer.

Catherine Abbey Hodges' most recent collection is *Raft of Days*. Best of the Net and Pushcart nominees, her poems appear widely and have been featured on *The Writer's Almanac* and *Verse Daily*.

Jeff Holt is the author of *The Harvest* (White Violet Press, 2012). He has previously published poems in *Measure*. He works as a Licensed Professional Counselor specializing in trauma issues.

Paul Hostovsky is the author of ten books of poetry; most recently, *Late for the Gratitude Meeting* (Kelsay Books, 2019). He makes his living in Boston as a sign language interpreter. paulhovstovsky.com

Nancy Jesse taught English for over thirty years at West High School, Madison, Wisconsin, where she worked with the mentor and friend who plays the starring role in her villanelle.

A. M. Juster, the author of nine books, is the poetry editor of *First Things*. His work has appeared in *Poetry, Paris Review, Hudson Review,* and many other journals.

Julie Kane's doctoral dissertation was titled "How the Villanelle's Form Got Fixed." Her next poetry collection, *Mothers of Ireland,* is forthcoming from LSU Press in the fall of 2020.

Karen Kelsay has been published in numerous journals. Six of her poems have been nominated for a Pushcart Prize. She won the Fluvanna Prize from *The Lyric Magazine,* and in 2012 received the Association for Mormon Letters Award.

Brian Jerrold Koester is a Pushcart Prize nominee and a Best of the Net Anthology nominee. His chapbook, *Bossa Nova,* is published by River Glass Books.

Amy Lemmon is the author of *The Miracles* and *Saint Nobody*. She is Professor and Chairperson of English and Communication Studies at the Fashion Institute of Technology and lives in New York City.

Barbara Loots occasionally ventures from home in Kansas City, Missouri. Her poems are collected in *Road Trip* (2014) and *Windshift* (2018), both from Kelsay Books.

Eileen Mattmann's poetry was nominated for Best of the Net 2018, and has appeared in *Riddled With Arrows, Millwork, Postcard Poems and Prose,* and others.

Janet McCann is an old Texas poet who taught at Texas A&M for 46 years. Her last book is *The Crone at the Casino* (Lamar U Press, 2014).

Susan McLean's books of poetry include *The Best Disguise* and *The Whetstone Misses the Knife,* as well as *Selected Epigrams,* her translations of Latin poems by Martial.

Richard Merelman is Professor Emeritus of Political Science, University of Wisconsin–Madison. He has published a volume of poetry, *The Imaginary Baritone,* and chapbooks *The Unnamed Continent* and *Sensorium*. He and his wife live in Madison.

Mary Meriam co-founded Headmistress Press and edits *Lavender Review* (lesbian poetry and art). She's the author of *The Lillian Trilogy* (2015) and *My Girl's Green Jacket* (2018).

Leslie Monsour has received five Pushcart nominations and an NEA Fellowship. Her most recent collection is *The House Sitter* (Finishing Line Press). She resides in Los Angeles, California.

Burt Myers works as an art director in upstate New York. He's had poems published recently in *The Hopkins Review, Barrow Street, Tar River Poetry,* and elsewhere.

Chris O'Carroll is the author of *The Joke's on Me*. His poems appear in *New York City Haiku, The Great American Wise Ass Poetry Anthology,* and other collections.

Angela Alaimo O'Donnell is the author of two chapbooks and five collections of poems; most recently, *Still Pilgrim*. Her new collection, *Andalusian Hours: Poems from the Porch of Flannery O'Connor,* is forthcoming.

Jenifer Reeser's poems, literary criticism, essays, and translations of Russian, French, Cherokee and various Native American languages, appear widely. Her sixth poetry collection, *Indigenous*, is forthcoming from Able Muse Press.

Richard Roe, Middleton, Wisconsin, has published three books of poems, including *Bringer of Songs*. His work has appeared in periodicals, anthologies, and *Wisconsin Poets' Calendars*.

Jane Satterfield's most recent book is *Apocalypse Mix*, winner of the 2016 Autumn House Poetry Prize, selected by David St. John.

Wendy Sloan's poems and translations appear in *Able Muse, Light, Measure, Raintown Review, Think,* and several U.S. and UK anthologies. Her collection is *Sunday Mornings at the Caffe Mediterraneum* (2016).

David Southward teaches in the Honors College at the University of Wisconsin–Milwaukee. His first chapbook is *Apocrypha* (Wipf & Stock, 2018). davidsouthward.com

Susan Delaney Spear teaches at Colorado Christian University and is the Managing Editor of *Think*. Her collection of poems, *Beyond All Bearing*, was published by Wipf and Stock in 2017.

Andrew Szilvasy has poems appearing or forthcoming in *CutBank, Smartish Pace,* and *Barrow Street*, among others. He lives in Boston with his wife. When not reading or writing, he spends his time running, and brewing beer.

Judith Terzi lives in Pasadena, California, with her husband and her cockatiel, Gris-Gris. She is the author of *Museum of Rearranged Objects* (Kelsay Books, 2018) and five chapbooks.

Pat Valdata is a poet and novelist who lives in Crisfield, Maryland.

Kathrine Varnes, hatcher of improbable schemes, is the author of *The Paragon* and co-editor with Annie Finch of the popular *An Exaltation of Forms*. She teaches at the Fashion Institute in Manhattan.

Wendy Videlock lives on the western slope of the Colorado Rockies. Her most recent book, *Slingshots and Love Plums*, is available from Able Muse Press.

Lisa Vihos is the poetry editor of *Stoneboat* and the Sheboygan, Wisconsin, organizer for 100 Thousand Poets for Change. Her fourth chapbook is *Fan Mail from Some Flounder* (Main Street Rag Publishing, 2018). lisavihos.com

Ed Werstein, a Regional VP of the Wisconsin Fellowship of Poets, received the Council for Wisconsin Writers 2018 Lorine Niedecker Prize for Poetry.

Lesley Wheeler's poetry collections include *Radioland* and the chapbook *Propagation*. She teaches at Washington and Lee in Lexington, Virginia, and is the poetry editor of *Shenandoah*.

Gail White writes and feeds cats in Breaux Bridge, Louisiana. Her books *Asperity Street* and *Catechism* are available on Amazon. She is a contributing editor to *Light*.

www.ingramcontent.com/pod-product-compliance
Lightning Source LLC
LaVergne TN
LVHW091317080426
835510LV00007B/532